Animals with Jobs

Hearing Dogs

Judith Janda Presnall

KIDHAVEN PRESS

An imprint of Thomson Gale, a part of The Thomson Corporation

THOMSON
™
GALE

Detroit • New York • San Francisco • San Diego • New Haven, Conn. • Waterville, Maine • London • Munich

To Jilla

Acknowledgments
I appreciate the efforts of the following people who read
my manuscript for accuracy and made helpful suggestions:

Robin Dickson, President and CEO
Dogs for the Deaf, Inc., Central Point, Oregon

Martha A. Foss, Chairman and Executive Director
International Hearing Dog, Inc., Henderson, Colorado

Ralph Dennard, Director
Martha Hoffman, Dog Trainer and Author of *Lend Me an Ear*
San Francisco SPCA Hearing Dog Program, San Francisco, California

LIBRARY OF CONGRESS CATALOGING-IN-PUBLICATION DATA

Presnall, Judith Janda.
    Hearing dogs / byJudith Janda Presnall.
        p. cm. — (Animals with Jobs)
    Includes bibliographical references and index.
    Summary: Describes the breeding, training, and work done by hearing dogs for the deaf.
    ISBN 0-7377-1826-9 (hardback : alk. paper)
    1. Hearing dogs. 2. Dog trainers. [1. Hearing dogs. 2. Dogs.] I. Title. II. Series

Contents

Chapter One

An Extra Pair of Ears

Trained hearing dogs assist people who are deaf or hearing **impaired**. The dogs serve as their partner's ears when they signal their owners to the ordinary household sounds they might not hear. Common sounds a dog is trained to respond to include a knock on a door, a chiming doorbell, an alarm clock, and a ringing telephone. Other noises that are important include blaring smoke and fire alarms, the buzzing or beeping timers on the oven and microwave, and a baby's cry. A hearing dog is also trained to alert to outdoor sounds such as sirens, honking horns, or shouts by jumping on or standing in front of its owner.

Providing Security

Hearing dogs increase the security, **independence**, and confidence of a deaf person. When a hearing dog hears something, it physically touches its owner to alert him or her to sounds. The trained dogs signal by nudging their masters with their nose or paws, and then running to the sound. Sometimes the dogs even jump on their partners if they are slow to respond.

Hearing dogs help people who are deaf or hard of hearing by giving them companionship and a chance to lead safe, independent lives.

For example, Taj Brumleve and her three-year-old daughter Alexandra are both deaf. Her hearing dog is named Ivan. One afternoon Taj put her daughter down for a nap and went downstairs to stretch out on the couch. Ivan lay on the floor next to her. Taj had fallen asleep when she suddenly felt the huge husky on her chest. Ivan was licking her face and frantically pawing her arm.

The drowsy Taj pushed Ivan off and started to drift back to sleep. Then she remembered that Ivan would not jump on her unless something was wrong. When she opened her eyes, Ivan was gone and the room was foggy with smoke. Taj leaped off the couch and raced toward the stairs to get Alexandra. At the bottom of the stairs she met Ivan, tugging the sleepy Alexandra by her shirtsleeve toward the front door. The dog had saved both mother and daughter from a disastrous home fire.

How Training Dogs for the Deaf Began

Hearing dogs have been alerting people with hearing impairments for more than twenty-five years. The first organized effort to train hearing dogs began in 1974. A deaf woman came to a kennel in Lake Elmo, Minnesota, where dog trainer Agnes McGrath was working as kennel manager. The visitor asked if a hearing dog could be trained for her. She had owned a dog that she herself trained to alert her, but it had died of old age.

When the local Lions Club offered their financial support for a hearing dog project, McGrath accepted the challenge. She trained and placed about a half-dozen dogs with hearing-impaired people in Minnesota. A year

Training a hearing dog begins when the dog is a puppy.

later, the American Humane Association (AHA) took over the project from the Lions Club. McGrath and the AHA received a grant to conduct a four-year pilot (experimental) study in Colorado.

Others Get Involved

The AHA invited Roy Kabat, an animal trainer for the movies, to Colorado, seeking his ideas for the best ways to train hearing dogs. Kabat was so enthusiastic about the program that he returned home to start his own training center. In 1977, Kabat founded the first hearing dog training center, Dogs for the Deaf, in Jacksonville, Oregon.

Two years later, Agnes McGrath, along with three other female partners, opened Hearing Dog, Inc., in Henderson, Colorado. To date, these two organizations have trained and placed more than sixteen hundred dogs to assist the deaf throughout the United States and Canada. Approximately three dozen facilities, including six in foreign countries, now train dogs to be the ears of hearing-impaired people.

The cost of training and placing a hearing dog varies from one program to another, but averages fif-

Before they are placed with a partner, hearing dogs live with their trainer and learn verbal and hand signals.

Hearing Dogs Welcome Here

The Americans with Disabilities Act, passed by Congress in 1990, allows hearing dogs and their handlers to go into all public places such as:

- Airplanes
- Buses
- Hotels
- Office Buildings
- Movie Theaters
- Restaurants
- Sports Facilities
- Stores
- Trains

teen thousand dollars. Most training facilities place hearing dogs free of charge to qualified applicants. However, once placed, financial responsibility for the ongoing care of the dog is up to its owner.

The Americans with Disabilities Act, passed by the U.S. Congress in 1990, allows certified hearing dogs to go with their owners into all public facilities, just like guide dogs for the blind.

Deafness Changes Way of Life

Deafness is a disability that is not always apparent to strangers. They may not realize that the person cannot hear sounds such as approaching traffic, passing sirens, or another person's warning shout.

However, deaf persons can be aware of their environment by using other senses: sight, smell, touch, and taste. In addition, most people are not totally deaf and can hear certain sounds.

Some people are born with hearing impairments, while others lose their hearing later in life. One day, Susanne Bergeron had a ringing in her ears, and the next day she was nearly deaf due to a rare inner ear disease. As each day passed, it became more difficult for her to be a part of the hearing world she had known. She could not hear traffic noises and while walking was almost struck by passing trucks or cars several times.

"Being deaf is very lonely at times and very frustrating,"[1] Susanne says.

But that was before Susanne received her hearing dog, Yonkers, a black-and-white border collie. Now Susanne depends on Yonkers. The dog alerts her to noises such as the clothes dryer buzzing, someone calling her name, and traffic noises.

A Hearing Dog Is Better than a Vibrating Clock

Barbara Bird no longer uses a vibrating alarm clock under her pillow to wake her. She now has a hearing dog named Ceri to do that job. Barbara explains:

I have been severely deaf for the last thirty years. After my husband died I went through a period of feeling "like a ship without a sail." I was missing so many attempts by people to contact me by phone or at the door, and burnt food became my specialty. That is before I was given my hearing dog, Ceri. These days, her little face is the first thing I see in the morning. She jumps up to wake me when she hears the alarm—so much nicer than the vibrating clock under the pillow![2]

Michael Going tried using flashing lights to wake him from sleep, but they were totally ineffective. Now, with his trained border terrier–pug mix, Boonie, Michael never oversleeps.

A hearing dog wakes its partner when the alarm clock rings.

Dogs Provide Independence

Some people with hearing impairments do not feel safe when they are alone at home. That was the case with Doreen Feeney, who entered the world of complete silence when she suffered nerve deafness. The disorder made her hearing aids useless. However, since she obtained her two-year-old beagle mix named Charmin, Doreen no longer fears being alone. Charmin has also given peace of mind to Doreen's husband and two teenagers. They no longer worry about her safety when they leave the house.

Some children who are deaf are often lonely, and they sometimes suffer from fear of being trapped in a home fire. Twelve-year-old Matthew Jost has been deaf since birth. Matthew is somewhat isolated from other children because he is homeschooled. He wished he had a friend. Dogs for the Deaf gave him Lobo, a terrier mix. Lobo is his best friend. Matthew no longer worries about not hearing the smoke alarm. In addition, when Lobo hears Matthew's mother calling him, Lobo brings Matthew to her.

Not all dogs qualify for the special job of aiding the deaf. But many do, and most of them are found at animal shelters.

Which Dogs Qualify for Hearing Jobs?

Potential candidates for the job of hearing dog demand many of the same qualities as other working dogs. Like guide dogs and service dogs, hearing dogs must be friendly, behave well in public, and have an easygoing **temperament**. They must **bond** with their partner and want to please. Most training centers select their dogs from animal shelters. Hearing dog organizations are especially proud of two results of their work: rescuing dogs and helping people.

Rachael Hand, who is on the kennel staff of International Hearing Dog, Inc., says, "I have a deep sense of pride knowing that these dogs were taken from an uncertain fate and placed with an individual that will love, nurture, and value them because they otherwise would not have the chance to hear without the ears of their dog."[3]

Most hearing dogs are young, energetic, friendly dogs that are rescued from animal shelters.

Factors for Choosing Dogs

The primary considerations when trainers choose dogs from shelters are size, age, and temperament. Some hearing-impaired people want a large dog, but most people request small to medium-sized dogs (ten to forty pounds). Average-sized dogs take up less space in a small apartment and fit better in public situations (under tables or airplane seats). Older people prefer them because they are easier to control and exercise.

Mixed Breeds

Many hearing dog programs use mostly mixed breeds because they are what are available in shelters. As trainers walk through an animal shelter looking at dogs in cages on each side of the aisle, they look for energetic and friendly dogs.

One nine-month-old terrier mix named Millie attracted a trainer's attention by giving a huge bark and jumping three feet into the air. The trainer chose her because she was enthusiastic, unafraid, and excited. It was fortunate for Millie since she was scheduled to be **euthanized** that day at the shelter. Millie was successfully trained and placed with a hearing-impaired night watchman—a happy ending for all concerned.

Hearing dogs must be affectionate, intelligent, and easygoing; behave well in public; and be eager to please their partners.

Screening Kennel Dogs

Trainers usually **screen** the dogs while they are still in the kennel. A dog must display both trust and affection toward the trainer. It cannot be fearful or **aggressive**. Tests are done both inside and outside the cage.

While the dog is inside the cage, the trainer wants the dog to be friendly and come to the front of the cage. Dogs show other signs of potential by barking for attention, acting excited and happy, and allowing the trainer to pet them.

Once the dog is taken out of the cage, the trainer observes other behaviors. The dog must allow itself to be leashed and handled—a push on the rear (for sit) or shoulders (for down). It must permit its mouth to be opened, touched, and examined without biting. Playing with the tester and having high food motivation (wanting all treats) are favorable signs. It should not be afraid of an umbrella popping open, mechanical toys, or stairs. In addition, the dog must permit its food bowl to be pulled away without becoming upset, and it should not be aggressive toward other dogs.

Sound Testing on Dogs

Because the dogs must be able to hear a variety of sounds at different pitches, their own hearing ability must be tested. A few breeds have a higher occurrence of hearing impairments, and those will probably be passed over at the kennel. These include dalmatians, Australian cattle dogs, English bull terriers, and mixes of these dogs. Dogs must show excitement, curiosity,

Some dogs, like dalmatians, frequently have hearing impairments, so they are not selected as hearing dogs.

and interest when they hear assorted sounds. If a dog is slow or just walks, lies, or sits during a sound test, it fails the test.

Dogs must have a happy personality. In making their choices, many trainers ask themselves whether they would enjoy having this dog as a pet.

Chosen for Training

If a dog passes these **preliminary** tests, it will be selected as a possible hearing dog. The trainer brings the chosen dog back to the training center for a medical examination. A **veterinarian** checks to make sure the dog is healthy. The vet's exam is extensive: eyes, ears,

Before training begins, a veterinarian checks the dog thoroughly to make sure it is healthy.

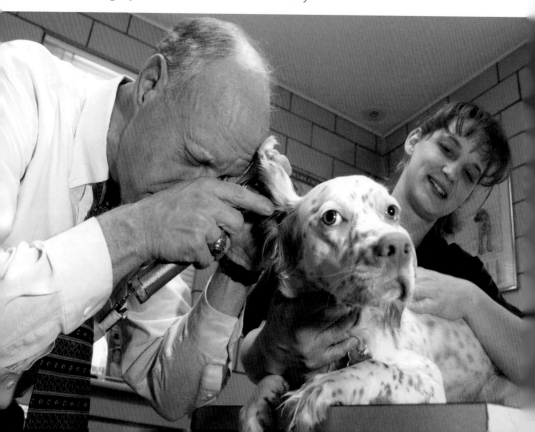

throat, teeth, heart, lungs, and temperature. After this basic exam, the veterinarian performs other procedures such as blood tests, vaccinations, and spaying or neutering before formal training begins.

A hearing dog fulfills three important functions in its job. It must be a well-behaved, trusting companion—a best friend. It must be comfortable in public situations. And the dog must react to sounds and alert its owner. The hearing dog links its deaf partner to the hearing world. Trainers must be confident that a dog can handle these duties and situations before they devote too much time to formal training.

Chapter Three

School Days

Ideal ages to train hearing dogs range from eight to twenty-four months. However, dogs that are five to seven years old can also be trained if they have the right temperament.

Dogs chosen from the shelter for hearing training are usually less than three years old. Dogs younger than eight months will be raised in a puppy raiser's home. Volunteer puppy raisers attend weekly classes where they learn methods of housebreaking and grooming their dogs. They learn to teach the dog basic obedience commands and how to walk with a leash. A puppy raiser also **socializes** his or her puppy by taking it to parks, shopping malls, restaurants, and other public places.

Methods vary between schools, but the goal is the same: train a dog to alert a hearing-impaired partner to sounds in his or her environment. Since attention span varies with the age and temperament of dog, the length

A hearing dog often becomes its partner's best friend.

of a training session depends on where the dog is in training. It can last anywhere from a few minutes to over an hour. Formal training lasts four to eight months. A hearing dog is trained in three areas: **sound awareness**, obedience, and socialization.

Sound Awareness

For teaching sound awareness, trainers use a furnished apartment, cottage, or rooms set up on the school grounds. These facilities are equipped with a bed, a tele-

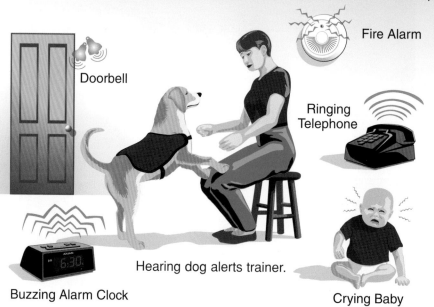

Sound Awareness Training

During sound awareness training, hearing dogs are trained to recognize different sounds such as a doorbell, a fire alarm, a ringing telephone, a crying baby, or a buzzing alarm clock and to alert the trainer by putting its paws in the trainer's lap.

Doorbell

Fire Alarm

Ringing Telephone

Hearing dog alerts trainer.

Buzzing Alarm Clock

Crying Baby

phone, an oven and microwave with timers, and possibly a baby crib with a "crying" (tape recorded) doll.

Mutual trust between the animal and trainer must be established before an animal will learn. The first step is for the trainers and dog to get to know each other. Usually two people work with the dog. They will set off a sound and watch the dog's reaction. They encourage the dog to run to the sound by running with the dog on a leash.

Next, the dog learns to alert the trainer when a sound is happening. The dog is taught to alert by putting its paws on the trainer's lap. The sound will be repeated, and each time the dog hears the sound, it should run to investigate it and then run to the trainer. When the dog responds correctly, the trainer rewards the dog with praise, a treat, or gives the dog a toy. The dog soon associates the sounds with rewards and begins to enjoy the act of alerting. If the dog fails to alert, the trainer repeats the exercise until the dog learns the lesson.

Alarm Clock Training

Vicky and Pete were student trainers in a hearing dog program. Vicky describes how they trained a dog named Buck to respond to the alarm clock:

> [Pete lay] down on the cot in the bedroom of the cottage and set the alarm clock while [I] waited in the next room with Buck on the leash. . . . When it rang, I jumped up and led Buck into the

bedroom, saying, "*Sound*, Buck! Tell Pete." At first Buck seemed reluctant to jump on the cot, but I encouraged him, and then we both petted and praised him.[4]

Buck learned quickly and soon was let off the leash. When Buck heard the alarm, he would dash into the bedroom, jump on the bed, and lick Pete's face to awaken him. During training, handlers use several different-sounding alarm clocks. In addition, the dog is taught to respond to doorbells by running to the door and then back to the trainer, bringing the person to the door. A variety of doorbells that ring, chime, or buzz are provided.

The dog is trained to signal to smoke or fire alarms by alerting its partner, going to the alarm, and sometimes leading him or her out of the building.

A Ringing Telephone

A dog also alerts to a ringing telephone by running back and forth between the telephone and its master. Hearing people may wonder how a deaf person uses a telephone. Some hard-of-hearing people have an **amplifier** on their telephone, and although they cannot hear the high-pitched ringing sound, they can usually understand the caller.

There are many people who are deaf and cannot hear even with an amplifier. These people oftentimes have a telecommunications device for the deaf called a TTY. The TTY is a text telephone, or teletype, with a keyboard and a small visual display of two to three lines. If a person with a TTY wants to call a hearing person who does not have a TTY, he or she would first call the state relay operator. This operator relays the conversation by speaking to the person called and by typing their response, which appears on the caller's TTY screen.

Many deaf or hard-of-hearing people use handheld wireless e-mail devices and text-message cell phones to communicate. However, none of these devices can replace an obedient hearing dog.

Obedience

Hearing dogs must be well behaved. Trainers work with the dogs on basic obedience commands such as "sit,"

Deaf people cannot use a regular telephone, but they can have a phone conversation if they use a text telephone, called a TTY.

Only about a third of the dogs that begin the training program successfully complete it and are placed in homes.

"come," "stay," "down," and "heel." Since many people who were born deaf prefer to use sign language, trainers teach the dogs both verbal and hand signals.

Socialization

A certified hearing dog must learn to be comfortable in crowds and fearless in traffic. It must behave well in restaurants, shopping malls, schools, places of employment, and any other place its partner goes. Getting a dog accustomed to these situations is called socialization.

Trainers also work on a dog's social skills twice a week by taking the dog out in public. If a dog fails at socialization, it will not be certified, although it can be placed as a home hearing dog—one that works only in the home.

Some Dogs Fail

Only one-third of the dogs are successful and complete the hearing dog training and placement program. Dogs that fail are usually released from the program because of temperament. They may not get along with small children. Some are nervous and jumpy in traffic and crowds. In some cases, however, they may be placed with a person who has unique needs that can be helped by having a trained, loving companion. All remaining dogs will be placed in homes where they are wanted and well cared for.

Applicants

To obtain a certified hearing dog, an applicant must be eighteen years old or older. In some programs, those applicants ages ten through seventeen may receive a hearing dog that works only in the home. However, rules relating to age vary from program to program. A deaf person who lives alone may have a higher priority for getting a hearing dog than someone who lives in a household with hearing people.

A hearing dog ordinarily will not be placed in a home where there is already a pet dog. In some cases, a deaf person would like to have his or her pet trained to alert to sounds. But most training centers refuse to do this because the dogs usually revert to being pets when they return to their home after training.

Applicants are interviewed in their home to evaluate their lifestyle, personality, special needs, and family environment. The applicant must submit a current

audiogram, which shows the degree of hearing loss. He or she must also be willing to maintain the dog's training. The hearing dog's training is tailored to a person's needs. When a center obtains a dog, trainers match and custom train the dog for a specific applicant.

Special Needs

If an applicant has a baby or small children in the home, the dog can be taught to respond to a crying baby or even to quarreling children. One example is the Smania family, in which both parents and their two daughters, ages eight and ten, have a severe or total hearing loss. When the two girls get into mischief or misbehave, the mother's hearing dog, named Ellie Mae, rushes off to alert her. It always surprises and puzzles the girls when their mom appears at the scene.

A Hearing Dog as a Partner

After the dog has completed formal training, some centers require the recipient to attend a weeklong class at their facility, where the person will be assigned a dog. Right away, he or she is responsible for feeding, walking, and grooming the dog. These tasks help form a bond of friendship that leads to the dog transferring its loyalty from trainer to recipient.

Other centers bring the custom-trained dog to the new owner's home. The trainer then spends up to five days helping the dog adjust and learn the sounds of that household. The trainer also instructs the recipient in dog care and how to maintain dog obedience and sound responses.

Who Qualifies for a Certified Hearing Dog?

To obtain a certified hearing dog,
an applicant must satisfy the following:

- be over eighteen years old*

- not have another dog in the home

- have at least a sixty-five decibel hearing loss

- be willing to maintain the hearing dog's training

- live alone or with other persons who are deaf or hard of hearing

* The age requirement may vary from program to program.

Gladys Peterson explains what happened when she received her hearing dog, Skipper, a long-haired dachshund mix, from Dogs for the Deaf:

Skipper's trainer [Peter] brought him to me by plane. He checked into a motel and brought Skipper to my house. . . . For five successive days, Peter came to my house and trained me. Skipper was already trained, but I had to learn to respond to him.

Hearing dogs can be trained to respond to a crying baby or even arguing children.

So we sounded the doorbell, the alarm clock, the smoke alarm, and the oven timer repeatedly. I asked friends to phone me as often as possible during the training sessions. At last, Peter decided I knew enough to leave Skipper with me permanently.[5]

After the dog and recipient have spent about ninety days bonding and practicing their skills together, trainers revisit the home. They test the dog and partner on their abilities to work as a team. If all is acceptable, the dog then becomes certified with an official identification card.

Chapter Four

Hearing Dogs on the Job

A hearing dog does not have the same advantages as other trained dogs. Guide dogs and service dogs respond to cues from a human. Instead of waiting for a command from the partner, a hearing dog must cue its human partner by its actions. In order to perform alerts on their own, hearing dogs must have exceptional intelligence and natural ability.

There are many examples of how hearing dogs instill confidence, help their partners on the job, and save lives.

Hero Dogs

Some hearing dogs become heroes when they rescue people from urgent or unsafe situations. In one instance, "[A woman named] Carol lay on the kitchen floor doubled over in pain. Her husband couldn't hear her screams, but their dog, Sasha, could. Sasha yanked the deaf man out of bed and led him to his wife in time to get her to the hospital, where she recovered from a heart attack."[6]

A young mother recalls the time she was alone at home with her baby and her hearing dog Sufi:

I was working in the back bedroom when Sufi ran into the room and jumped up, placing her paws upon me. I knew that was my cue to follow her. She brought me to the living room, where

Types of Assistance Dogs

- **Hearing dogs** are trained to alert deaf or hard-of-hearing individuals to sounds such as the telephone, smoke alarm, alarm clock, doorbell, or an ambulance siren.

- **Guide dogs** are trained to assist people who are blind or nearly blind to safely navigate their environment.

- **Service dogs** are trained to assist people who have a physical disability or a seizure disorder. Service dogs can open cupboards, retrieve items, or signal an oncoming seizure.

- **Rescue dogs** are trained to help save lives by finding missing people in disasters such as earthquakes, avalanches, train wrecks, or plane crashes.

the baby had fallen over in her walker. I don't know how long it would have taken me to discover the baby without Sufi. I know that I can count on my hearing-ear dog.[7]

Janice, another young mother, has been hard of hearing for more than twenty years. Janice's three-year-old daughter needed to be on a heart monitor at night in case her breathing or heart rate slowed to a dangerous level. Janice's hearing dog, a black cocker mix named Jo Jo, slept by the child's bed and monitor. On a

Hearing dogs are trained to alert their partners if the doorbell rings or if a smoke or fire alarm goes off.

particularly bad night, the monitor went off twenty-five times. Jo Jo alerted Janice each time!

Having Faith in Hearing Dogs

Krystyna explains that her retriever mix, Houston, has a busy life with his deaf family of five:

> We are very glad to have our hearing dog, Houston, because we are unable to hear most of the signals in our home. We have tried some of the equipment, but find that when the system breaks down or the power is out, we have nothing to back us up. . . . Houston doesn't break and doesn't need any electricity![8]

There are different requirements for dogs that work inside the home and those that work outside the home.

Hearing Dogs Outside the Home

Outside the home, the hearing dog wears its identification tag, orange collar, leash, and vest. Its human partner carries the dog's photo identification card. Some stores or restaurants are unwilling to allow dogs inside, but the law requires it. Nellie Lee describes her restaurant experience with her hearing dog Matt:

> One night we went to a restaurant for dinner. The manager was reluctant to have us, but did seat us. After eating, we were leaving when the manager came to us and said, "Lady, come back anytime. Do you think Matt's trainer might take some of the children who come in here and train them?"[9]

Hearing Dogs Help Partners at Their Jobs

One woman said that before she had a hearing dog, her coworkers used to throw erasers at her to get her attention. Now when they want her attention, they just call her name and her dog alerts her.

Sarah, a special education teacher's aide who is hard of hearing, has her students knock on their desks when they need her. Her hearing dog, Sadie, hears the knock and takes her to that child.

Diane Purdon tells how her hearing dog Tucker helps at her own business: "One day I was working at my desk . . . when Tucker went running out into the store, came back, hit me, and took me to the front door. It had locked by accident and a customer was knocking to get in."[10]

Changes in Assignment

If a human partner dies or for some other reason can no longer keep his or her hearing dog, several options are considered. If the dog is young enough to be placed again, the training facility will take the dog back, review its training, and place it with another applicant.

If the dog is too old or not healthy enough to work with another partner, it will be retired in a good home where it will receive the loving care it needs and deserves.

Sometimes organizations leave the dog with the family because the spouse or family members have a strong bond with the dog, and it is in the people's and dog's best interest for the dog to remain there.

Placements are not always successful. Student trainer Vicky gives an example of a dog that had to be returned to the training center:

Occasionally, a dog is returned to us because the situation just didn't work out. A teenage girl had to give back her dog last year. Her mother didn't really like dogs, we suspected, and was not supportive of the dog in the household. The girl was often negligent about taking care of her valuable helpmate, and the mother refused to. Finally, the father insisted that for the dog's sake it should be returned. . . . We placed the animal very soon with another deaf person.[11]

Hearing dogs connect their partners with the hearing world by giving them independence and companionship.

Ellen Raines summed up the feelings of most hearing dog recipients when she wrote to Dogs for the Deaf about her dog, Meko, a small, wispy-haired and droopy-eared mongrel: "She is a necessity, not a luxury. . . . I thank God for the loving gift of Meko. . . . I am so thankful for the special people like you who have taught me it's okay to be deaf—now I can be me instead of pretending to be something I wasn't."[12]

The gift of a hearing dog connects those who are deaf or hard of hearing to a hearing world. This special dog gives them independence, companionship, and the ability to lead safer and more self-reliant lives.

Notes

Chapter One: An Extra Pair of Ears
1. Quoted in "Graduate Profile," *Canine Companions for Independence: The Courier,* Summer 1998, p. 3.
2. Quoted in "Our Recipients," *Hearing Dogs for Deaf People,* www. hearing-dogs.co.uk.

Chapter Two: Which Dogs Qualify for Hearing Jobs?
3. Quoted in Valerie Foss-Brugger, "Meet Our Terrific Kennel Staff!" *International Hearing Dog, Inc.: Paws for Silence,* Spring 2000, p. 5.

Chapter Three: School Days
4. Quoted in Patricia Curtis, *Animal Partners: Training Animals to Help People.* New York: Dutton, 1982, p. 86.
5. Gladys Peterson, "Skipper," *The Best of Dogs for the Deaf,* December 1996, p. 124.

Chapter Four: Hearing Dogs on the Job
6. Franca Lebow, "Hearing Ear Dogs," *Health,* April 1985, p. 21.
7. Quoted in Mark Watts, "Now for the Deaf—Hearing-Ear Dogs," *Prevention,* April 1986, p. 10.
8. Quoted in "Comments from Satisfied Hearing Dog Owners," *International Hearing Dog, Inc.,* Summer 2001, p. 2.

9. Nellie Lee, "Ears to You," *Dogs for the Deaf: Canine Listener,* Winter 1997, p. 9.

10. Diane Purdon, "Ears to You," *Dogs for the Deaf: Canine Listener,* Spring 1996, p. 11.

11. Quoted in Curtis, *Animal Partners,* pp. 89–90.

12. Quoted in Carole Wilson, "Meko Expands Horizons," *The Best of Dogs for the Deaf,* December 1996, p. 97.

Glossary

aggressive: Quick to attack.

amplifier: An attachment to make the telephone louder.

audiogram: A graph showing the percentage of hearing loss in a particular ear as indicated by an audiometer.

bond: To become closer to someone through loyalty, caring, and love.

euthanized: The act of killing someone or something painlessly; a painless death.

impaired: Something that is flawed, damaged, or injured.

independence: Freedom; to take care of oneself without any help.

preliminary: Prior to other work or action.

screen: To examine or test and remove those that are unqualified.

socializes: Trains a dog to take part in activities with many people around.

sound awareness: A reaction to noises.

temperament: A manner of behaving and reacting.

veterinarian: One trained and authorized to treat animals medically.

Organizations to Contact

Dogs for the Deaf, Inc.
10175 Wheeler Rd.
Central Point, OR 97502
(541) 826-9220 voice/TDD
www.dogsforthedeaf.org
This organization chooses their dogs for training from adoption shelters and places hearing dogs throughout the United States and Canada.

International Hearing Dog, Inc.
5901 E. 89th Ave.
Henderson, CO 80640
(303) 287-3277 voice/TTY
www.IHDI.org
Adopting dogs from shelters, this organization trains and places hearing dogs with persons who are deaf or hard of hearing throughout the world.

San Francisco SPCA
Hearing Dog Program
2500 Sixteenth St.
San Francisco, CA 94103
(415) 554-3020
www.sfspca.org

The hearing dog program began in 1978 and offers assistance to deaf and hard-of-hearing individuals. The program also gives previously homeless animals a chance for useful lives of love and service.

For Further Exploration

Books

Patricia Curtis, *Cindy, a Hearing Ear Dog.* New York: E.P. Dutton, 1981. This book describes adopting a dog from a shelter, training it to be a hearing dog, and assigning it to a young deaf girl.

Peg Kehret, *Shelter Dogs.* Morton Grove, IL: Albert Whitman, 1999. This book tells the stories of eight dogs that were adopted from an animal shelter and went on to become service dogs, actors, and heroes.

Periodical

Jack Fincher, "A Mutt Named Meko," *Reader's Digest*, May 1990. This article describes a woman who was lost in a world of deafness and despair until she applied for and received a hearing dog.

Index

Picture Credits

Cover image: © Penny Tweedy/Science Photo Library
AP/Wide World Photos, 7, 8, 14, 15, 18
© Chapman/The Image Works, 26
Corel, 17
Chris Jouan, 22
Ken Lax/Photo Researchers, Inc., 25
© Michael Newman/Photo Edit, 34
© Frank Siteman/Index Stock Imagery, 5, 11
© Frank Siteman/Photo Edit, 21, 37
Penny Tweedie/Photo Researchers, Inc., 30

About the Author

Judith Janda Presnall is an award-winning nonfiction writer. *Hearing Dogs* is the twelfth book in her Animals with Jobs series. Some of her other books for children and young adults include *Life on Alcatraz, Oprah Winfrey, Animals That Glow,* and *Mount Rushmore.* She is a member of the Society of Children's Book Writers and Illustrators and the California Writers Club. The former high school teacher lives in the Los Angeles area with her husband Lance and three cats.